Animals of the Night

CAPYBARAS AFTER DARK

Heather M. Moore Niver

Enslow Publishing
101 W. 23rd Street
Suite 240
New York, NY 10011
USA

enslow.com

Words to Know

bacteria—Organisms that have only one cell.

dominant—Most important or powerful.

feces—Solid waste from the body.

herbivores—Animals that eat only plants.

mammals— Animals that have a backbone and hair, usually give birth to live babies, and produce milk to feed their young.

nocturnal—Mostly active at night.

predators—Animals that kill and eat other animals to stay alive.

prey—An animal hunted by another animal for food.

regurgitate—To move swallowed food back up into the mouth.

semiaquatic—Living near and spending time in the water, but not living in it.

Contents

Capybara Nights

Night falls on another hot day in South America. The sun sets and the day cools. The capybara stretches and peers around. Is it safe to look for food? After a day resting and keeping cool, the capybara is hungry. The coast is clear. So it's time to move from the mud and water. It walks inland and starts to chow down. The capybara grazes on grass and plants near the water all night long. When the sun comes back up, the capybara settles down for the day.

Capybaras will spend almost all night munching and grazing.

Related to Rodents

Capybaras are **mammals** that live in Central and South America. They are also called carpinchos or water hogs. Capybaras are the largest rodents in the world. When they stand, capybaras are almost 2 feet (60 centimeters) tall at the shoulder. Capybaras are about 3 to 4 feet (100 to 130 cm) long. They hardly have any tail at all. This stocky animal weighs around 60 to 174 pounds (27 to 79 kilograms). Males tend to be heavier than females. Capybaras are cousins to guinea pigs and chinchillas.

FUN FACT!

Capybaras lived in North America during the Ice Age. Human hunting probably killed them off in that area 10,000 years ago.

Capybaras are the biggest rodents around. They are almost 2 feet (60 cm) tall.

Capybaras are stout animals. They have a short head and nose. Their legs are quite short. Their bodies are covered with short thick fur. Their fur can be brown, yellow, red, or gray.

Capybaras have small ears. Their ears, eyes, and nostrils are located on the tops of the heads. They can keep most of their body underwater when they need to. This comes in handy when they are hiding from danger.

FUN FACT!

Hippopotamuses hide with only their ears, eyes, and nostrils above water, too, but they are not related to capybaras.

It's handy to have eyes, ears, and a nose on top of your head.
This helps to hide in the water.

Capybaras have four feet. Their front feet have four toes with webs in between them. Their back feet only have three toes. A capybara's back feet do not have webs, though. Toes have a tough claw that is kind of like a hoof.

Sometimes capybaras like to hang out sitting up. They will sit on their back feet. Unlike other rodents, they cannot use their front feet to hold food. So they have to wait to have a snack.

The capybara's front feet have four toes. The webs help them swim.

Oh, the Water

Capybaras are **semiaquatic**. This means they spend a lot of time in the water (but they don't live in it). They have dry skin, so they always live near water to keep it moist. Capybaras live near rivers, ponds, marshes, and other bodies of water.

Capybaras can stay underwater for up to five minutes. This helps them hide from **predators** if they need to. They press their ears against their heads when they are underwater.

FUN FACT!

Capybaras can run fast on land, especially when they are scared and want to escape. They run straight for the water!

Capybaras are great swimmers, but they are also skilled divers.

Capybaras get most of their food in the water. They are **herbivores**. They eat only vegetables, such as grass and other plants. Many of these grow in the water. They also like to eat melons, grains, and squash when water plants are not available.

In one day a capybara can eat up to 6 to 8 pounds (3 to 3 ½ kg) of fresh grass. Sometimes they even eat their own **feces**. These droppings have important **bacteria** that help them break down all that grass.

FUN FACT!

Even though they eat a lot, capybaras are picky eaters. Most of what they eat comes from the same few plants.

Capybaras eat a lot of plants that grow in the water.

Like their rodent relatives, capybaras have very large front teeth. These teeth are handy for cutting through grass and plants. Their teeth are always growing. Chewing on sticks and rough leaves helps their teeth from getting too long. Capybaras have twenty teeth.

Capybaras chow down using a side-to-side motion. (Humans chew up and down.) This way of chewing is great for breaking down leaves. Chewing is a very important task for capybaras. To make sure their food is perfectly ready to digest, they **regurgitate** it. This means they chew, swallow, and then chew it again.

FUN FACT!

Sheep, cows, and giraffes are other animals that regurgitate their food.

Capybaras have large front teeth. The teeth are always growing, and chewing helps keep them from getting too long.

Chill Capybaras

Capybaras like to chill out. They don't sleep that much. Instead of sleeping they like to doze and rest all day. Capybaras rest in the shade, mud, or water. During the day it is hot, so this helps them keep cool. In the evening, they finally get up to eat.

Capybaras are **nocturnal**. This means they are most active at night. They head inland to eat almost all night long. Capybaras are more strictly nocturnal in areas where they live near humans.

FUN FACT!

Capybaras will wait in a good hiding spot until dark if they think there is danger around.

Capybaras enjoy resting and dozing. But they really do not sleep too much.

Crowds of Capys

Capybaras are social animals. They like to hang out with groups, or herds, of other capys. In most groups, one **dominant** male leads a group of females, other males, and young. Groups are usually made up of between ten and thirty animals. When water is hard to find, more than forty capybaras may gather together.

Hanging out in groups is useful. This means lots of capybaras can watch the young. They can also keep an eye out for predators.

FUN FACT!

Capybara young have to beware of caimans, ocelots, harpy eagles, and anacondas. Adults are usually **prey** to jaguars. Humans hunt them, too.

Capybaras love to hang out in large groups known as herds.

Different herds of capybaras will sometimes live very near each other. But each herd has a certain area where they graze. If capys from another herd are found in their spot, they will be chased away!

Capybaras talk a lot! They make all kinds of sounds. For example, they yelp, bark, chirp, whistle, huff, and growl. When danger comes around they bark a warning. An entire herd will bark until the danger moves away! Young capybaras will purr and whistle if they get separated from their herd.

Capybaras live in herds. They communicate with each other using lots of different sounds.

Capybaras also communicate using smell. Adults mark their special areas with scent glands near their tails. Other capybaras will know this is another herd's area.

Male capybaras also have a special scent gland called a morillo. It is a dark spot found on the top of his nose. It doesn't have any fur on it. A thick, white, sticky substance comes out of it. The dominant male will use this scent to tell other capybaras that he's in charge.

FUN FACT!

Male capybaras walk over plants to leave their scent there. Sometimes they make sure to leave their scent on the females, too!

A male capybara lets others know who is in charge with scent from a morillo on his nose.

Baby Capys

Only the dominant male gets to be the father in a herd. Most of the time, females get pregnant in April or May. It can happen at any time, though. They mate right in the water. After five or six months, the female has her babies on land. Mama goes off to a quiet spot to give birth. She might have between one and eight babies at a time. Baby capybaras are called pups. A few hours after she gives birth, the mother joins her herd again.

Usually, a female only has one litter of babies a year.

Pups have fur and can see when they are born. They can run, swim, and even dive within hours, too! At first they only drink milk. Within a week after birth they are chomping on grass and other plants, too.

A group of pups from a herd is called a crèche. The crèche stays together while they are young. They drink milk from any female who is nursing, or providing milk. All the females in the group help take care of all the young.

Baby capybaras, called pups, can run, swim, and dive soon after they are born.

Stay Safe Around Capybaras

Capybaras may seem like relaxed friendly animals. But remember that capybaras are wild animals. Here are some safety tips in case you ever come face to face with a capybara:

- Never try to keep a wild capybara as a pet. They can be aggressive and sometimes bite with their sharp teeth!

- Capybaras will make a clicking sound to warn off threats. If you hear a capybara making this noise, leave it alone.

- Some people keep capybaras as pets. Where capybaras are legal, there are rules about how to care for them. They need a large amount of space and a good-sized swimming area all year round to live happily. If they are unhappy they can get aggressive and dangerous.

Learn More

Books

Borgert-Spaniol, Megan. *Capybaras*. Minneapolis: Bellwether Media, 2014.

Lynette, Rachel, and Marc C. Anderson. *Capybaras*. New York: Bearport Publishing, 2013.

Schaefer, Susan. *Capybaras*. New York: Cavendish Square Publishing, 2015.

Websites

A–Z Animals: Capybara

a-z-animals.com/animals/capybara/
Check out capybara photos, facts, and maps.

San Diego Zoo: Capybara

animals.sandiegozoo.org/animals/capybara
Photos and facts teach you all about capybara life.

Rainforest Alliance: Capybara

www.rainforest-alliance.org/kids/species-profiles/ capybara
Get more information about capybaras.

Index

Published in 2017 by Enslow Publishing, LLC.
101 W. 23rd Street, Suite 240, New York, NY 10011

Copyright © 2017 by Enslow Publishing, LLC.
All rights reserved.

No part of this book may be reproduced by any means without the
written permission of the publisher.

Library of Congress Cataloging-in-Publication Data
Names: Niver, Heather Moore, author.
Title: Capybaras after dark / Heather M. Moore Niver.
Other titles: Animals of the night.
Description: New York, NY : Enslow Publishing, 2017 | Series: Animals
of the night | Includes bibliographical references and index.
Identifiers: LCCN 2015044906| ISBN 9780766077065 (library
bound) | ISBN 9780766077331 (pbk.) | ISBN 9780766076815
(6-pack)
Subjects: LCSH: Capybara—Behavior—Juvenile literature. | Nocturnal
animals—Juvenile literature.
Classification: LCC QL737.C4 N58 2016 | DDC 599.35/9—dc23
LC record available at http://lccn.loc.gov/2015044906

Printed in the United States of America

To Our Readers: We have done our best to make sure all website
addresses in this book were active and appropriate when we went to
press. However, the author and the publisher have no control over and
assume no liability for the material available on those websites or on any
websites they may link to. Any comments or suggestions can be sent by
e-mail to customerservice@enslow.com.

Photo Credits: Throughout book, narvikk/E+/Getty Images (starry
background), kimberrywood/Digital Vision Vectors/Getty Images
(green moon dingbat); cover , p. 1 Danita Delimont/Gallo Images/
Getty Images, samxmed/E+/Getty Images (moon); pp. 3, 21, 25 Vadim
Petrakov/Shutterstock.com; p. 5 Viktor Čáp/iStock/Thinkstock; p.
7 DrMonochrome/iStock/Thinkstock; p. 9 Erni/Shutterstock.com;
p. 11 TOMO/Shutterstock.com; pp. 13, 15, 23 Wolfgang Kaehler/
LighRocket/Getty Images; p. 17 nastenkin/iStock/Thinkstock; p. 19
Ricardokuhl/Shutterstock.com; p. 27 NELSON ALMEIDA/AFP/
Getty Images; p. 29 ullstein bild/Getty Images.